ISBN: 9798305765199

AI for Beginners

Unlock the Power of Artificial Intelligence to Turbocharge Your Life and Career

TABLE OF CONTENTS

Introduction

Welcome to the exciting world of Artificial Intelligence (AI)! If you've picked up this book, chances are you're curious about AI and how it's shaping the world around us. Maybe you've heard about ChatGPT, robots that can paint like Picasso, or apps that seem to know what you want before you do. Whatever brought you here, you're in for an eye-opening journey.

Let's start with a little confession: AI can sound intimidating. Terms like "neural networks" and "machine learning" might make you think of science fiction movies or genius-level coders working in secret labs. But here's the truth—it doesn't have to be complicated. Think of AI as a really smart helper that's here to make your life easier, more productive, and even a little more fun.

Imagine this: You're planning a dinner party. AI can suggest recipes, create a shopping list, and even help you write a witty invitation for your friends. Or picture yourself at work, drowning in emails—AI can draft replies for you in seconds. It's like having an assistant who never takes a coffee break.

In this book, we'll break down the mysteries of AI into simple, digestible nuggets. No technical jargon, no long equations—just practical insights and easy-to-follow examples. By the end, you'll not only understand AI, but you'll also know how to use it to make your life and career a whole lot better.

Here's what's waiting for you:

- We'll demystify what AI actually is and how it works (without making your head spin).
- You'll discover real-life ways to use AI in your day-to-day life, from saving time to boosting your creativity.
- We'll introduce you to some of the coolest AI tools out there and show you how to get started with them.
- And because no one likes surprises, we'll talk about AI's limitations and how to use it responsibly.

This book is like a roadmap for your AI adventure. Whether you're a total beginner or just looking to stay ahead of the curve, you're in the right place. Ready to dive in? Great! Let's unlock the power of AI together and turbocharge your life and career.

01 Welcome to the World of AI

AI is everywhere. It's in your phone, your email inbox, and even your favorite shopping apps. But if you're like most people, you might not fully understand what it is or how it works—and that's okay! In this chapter, we're going to take a friendly stroll through the fascinating world of Artificial Intelligence, showing you how it's transforming everyday life and why it matters to you.

Why AI Matters

Think about the last time you used your smartphone. Maybe you asked Siri or Google Assistant for directions, used a fitness app to track your steps, or browsed Netflix for something new to watch. Every one of these interactions is powered by AI. But AI isn't just about convenience—it's shaping industries, changing careers, and even sparking debates about what the future might look like.

Here's why AI is so important:

- **It Saves Time**: AI can automate repetitive tasks, freeing you up for things you truly care about.
- **It Solves Problems**: From diagnosing diseases to optimizing traffic, AI tackles challenges that once seemed insurmountable.
- **It Unlocks Creativity**: With tools that help write, draw, and design, AI makes creative work accessible to everyone.
- **It Levels the Playing Field**: Small businesses and individuals now have access to tools once reserved for massive corporations.

How AI is Transforming Everyday Life

AI isn't just a buzzword—it's quietly (and sometimes not so quietly) reshaping the world around us. Let's explore some of the ways AI is revolutionizing everyday life:

- **Smart Assistants**: AI-powered helpers like Alexa and Siri have become our personal concierges, answering questions, setting reminders, and even controlling smart home devices. These assistants learn from your habits, making their suggestions more helpful over time.
- **Personalized Recommendations**: Ever wondered how Spotify knows your taste in music or how Amazon suggests exactly what you were thinking of buying? That's AI analyzing your preferences and predicting what you might like next. It's not just convenient—it makes discovering new things effortless.

- **Healthcare Breakthroughs**: AI is revolutionizing medicine, from early cancer detection to personalized treatment plans tailored to individual patients. AI-powered tools assist doctors in diagnosing conditions faster and more accurately, saving lives and improving outcomes.
- **Transportation Innovations**: Self-driving cars and AI-powered traffic systems are making our commutes safer and more efficient. Imagine a future where traffic jams are a thing of the past, thanks to AI systems optimizing traffic flow in real time.
- **Everyday Conveniences**: Whether it's a chatbot helping you return an online purchase or an AI camera identifying faces in photos, AI is working behind the scenes to simplify your life in countless ways. From automating routine tasks to enhancing personal experiences, AI is everywhere.

The Big Picture: Why Should You Care About AI?

So, why should you care about AI? Because it's not just a tool for techies—it's a game-changer for everyone. AI has the power to make your life easier, your work more efficient, and your creativity boundless. As we dive deeper into this book, you'll learn how AI can help you:

- **Be more productive**: Automate mundane tasks and focus on what truly matters.
- **Unleash your creativity**: Use AI to write, brainstorm, and design like never before.

- **Stay ahead in your career**: Understand AI's impact on industries and how you can leverage it to grow professionally.
- **Simplify your personal life**: From meal planning to organizing events, AI can make day-to-day living smoother and more enjoyable.

A Roadmap for What's Ahead

AI is no longer a futuristic concept—it's here, and it's already changing the way we live and work. But here's the exciting part: we're just scratching the surface. In the chapters ahead, we'll unpack what AI is, how it works, and how you can use it to unlock new opportunities in your life and career.

We'll explore everything from practical tools you can use today to visionary ideas about AI's future. Whether you're a tech enthusiast or someone who's just curious, this book will show you how to harness the power of AI to enhance your personal and professional life. So, let's dive in and see what the future holds!

02 What is Generative AI?

Artificial Intelligence—just hearing the term might make you think of robots, sci-fi movies, or even the end of the world. But let's bring it down to earth. What exactly is AI? And why is everyone talking about it?

Breaking Down the Buzzwords

At its core, AI is about creating systems that can perform tasks that would normally require human intelligence. Think of things like understanding language, recognizing patterns, solving problems, or making decisions. It's not magic—it's math, data, and a lot of clever programming.

Now, let's talk about **Generative AI**—one of the hottest topics in technology today. Generative AI doesn't just follow instructions; it creates. It can write a story, compose music, or generate images. Think of it as an artist who never runs out of inspiration, powered by algorithms and massive amounts of data. Unlike traditional AI, which focuses on analyzing and interpreting data, Generative AI pushes boundaries by creating something entirely new based on patterns it has learned.

Why AI is Dominating the News

AI has been around for decades, so why is it suddenly such a big deal? Two main reasons:

1. **Advances in Technology**: Computing power has skyrocketed, and access to vast amounts of data has enabled AI systems to become smarter and faster. Algorithms have improved, and the infrastructure for training complex models has become more accessible.
2. **Accessible Tools**: AI is no longer confined to research labs. Thanks to platforms like ChatGPT and image generators like DALL-E, anyone can use AI to solve problems, create content, or explore new ideas. What was once the domain of specialists is now available to students, entrepreneurs, and hobbyists alike.

But let's not forget the controversies. AI has sparked debates about ethics, privacy, and even job displacement. While these are important issues, they shouldn't overshadow the incredible potential AI has to improve our lives. From making tasks easier to expanding human creativity, AI is poised to be a transformative force.

Everyday Examples of AI in Action

To make AI less abstract, let's look at some everyday examples you might already be familiar with:

- **Email Filters**: Spam folders are powered by AI, sorting unwanted messages so you don't have to.
- **Streaming Services**: Netflix, YouTube, and Spotify recommend content tailored to your tastes, all thanks to AI analyzing your preferences.
- **Navigation Apps**: Google Maps and Waze use AI to provide real-time traffic updates and suggest the fastest routes.
- **Voice Assistants**: Alexa, Siri, and Google Assistant answer questions, set reminders, and even tell jokes, all powered by natural language processing (NLP).
- **E-commerce**: Amazon and other retailers suggest products you didn't know you needed, based on your browsing and purchase history.

Generative AI: A Closer Look

Generative AI takes things to the next level by creating entirely new content. Here are a few cool ways it's being used:

- **Writing and Creativity**: Tools like ChatGPT can draft emails, generate story ideas, or even help with homework. Authors and marketers alike use it to brainstorm and refine their content.
- **Art and Design**: Platforms like MidJourney and DALL-E create stunning visuals from simple text prompts, democratizing access to professional-grade design.

- **Business Applications**: Generative AI is being used to write reports, create presentations, and even generate marketing copy. Teams are saving hours by automating routine tasks while focusing on strategy and execution.
- **Education**: Generative AI is helping students learn by explaining complex concepts, summarizing textbooks, and even providing practice questions.

Why It's Important to Understand AI

Whether you're a student, a professional, or just someone who likes staying informed, understanding AI is becoming essential. Here's why:

- **It's Everywhere**: From your smartphone to your doctor's office, AI touches almost every aspect of life.
- **It's a Career Booster**: Knowing how to use AI tools can give you an edge in the workplace, helping you stand out as a tech-savvy problem solver.
- **It's Empowering**: The more you understand AI, the more you can use it to your advantage—whether that's saving time, learning something new, or tackling a big project.

The Ethical Side of AI

Understanding AI also means being aware of its ethical implications. As AI tools become more powerful, questions about privacy, bias, and accountability come to the forefront. For example:

- How do we ensure AI systems make fair and unbiased decisions?
- What happens to the data we input into AI tools?
- How can we use AI responsibly to minimize harm and maximize benefits?

These are complex questions, but they're essential for navigating the AI-powered future responsibly.

A World of Possibilities

So, what is AI? It's a helper, a creator, a problem-solver, and, yes, sometimes a disruptor. Generative AI, in particular, is opening doors to creativity and innovation that we've never seen before. The best part? You don't need a PhD in computer science to benefit from it. All you need is curiosity and a willingness to experiment.

In the next chapter, we'll take a step back and look at how AI got here, from its humble beginnings to the powerful tools we use today. Get ready for a quick and fascinating journey through the history of AI!

03 A Brief History of AI

Artificial Intelligence may feel like a 21st-century buzzword, but its roots stretch back much further. To understand how we got to today's powerful AI tools, we need to take a quick trip through time and look at the key milestones that brought us here.

The Early Days: AI as a Concept

The idea of intelligent machines has fascinated humanity for centuries. Ancient myths described mechanical beings brought to life, and in the 20th century, writers like Isaac Asimov popularized the idea of robots and artificial brains. But AI as a scientific pursuit officially began in the mid-20th century.

- **1950s**: Alan Turing, a brilliant mathematician, asked the groundbreaking question, "Can machines think?" He developed the Turing Test to evaluate whether a machine could mimic human intelligence convincingly. This question laid the foundation for AI as a field of inquiry.

- **1956**: The term "Artificial Intelligence" was coined at the Dartmouth Conference, marking the birth of AI as a formal field of study. Researchers began experimenting with basic programs capable of solving mathematical problems and playing games like chess.
- **1960s**: Early AI programs like ELIZA, a chatbot simulating human conversation, showcased the potential of machines to interact using natural language.

AI's Evolution: From Dreams to Applications

After its ambitious beginnings, AI went through cycles of enthusiasm and setbacks. Here's how it evolved:

- **1970s and 1980s: AI Winters**
  - Funding and interest in AI waned during these decades due to unmet expectations and limited computing power.
  - Despite this, foundational technologies like expert systems (programs designed to mimic human decision-making) kept the field alive. These systems were widely used in industries like medicine and engineering.
- **1990s: The Internet and Machine Learning**
  - The rise of the internet brought a surge of data—fuel for AI algorithms. More data meant better training opportunities for machine learning models.

- Machine learning, a subset of AI, began to shine, with systems learning from data rather than relying solely on programmed rules.
- **1997: A Landmark Moment**: IBM's Deep Blue made history by defeating world chess champion Garry Kasparov. This achievement captured global attention and demonstrated the potential of AI to outperform humans in specific tasks.

The AI Boom: 2000s to Today

With advances in computing power and the explosion of data, AI entered a new golden age in the 2000s. Some key breakthroughs include:

- **2000s: AI Goes Mainstream**
  - Google revolutionized search algorithms with AI, and platforms like Amazon began using AI for personalized recommendations. AI also started transforming industries, from finance to healthcare.
  - Robotics gained momentum, with advances in autonomous systems and the development of robots capable of performing specialized tasks.
- **2010s: Deep Learning and Big Data**
  - Deep learning, inspired by the structure of the human brain, enabled AI systems to process vast amounts of data and recognize patterns with unprecedented accuracy. This era saw the rise of convolutional neural networks, which became crucial for image recognition.

- Voice assistants like Siri, Alexa, and Google Assistant entered homes, showcasing AI's practical applications in everyday life.
  - AI-powered applications in healthcare advanced rapidly, enabling early detection of diseases and personalized treatments.
- **2020s: The Age of Generative AI**
  - Tools like ChatGPT and DALL-E brought generative AI to the masses, enabling users to create text, art, and more with simple prompts. These tools blurred the lines between human and machine creativity.
  - AI's integration into daily tools like email, navigation, and design made it more accessible to millions of users worldwide. Automation expanded into logistics, customer service, and content creation.

Fun Fact: Chess and AI

When IBM's Deep Blue defeated Garry Kasparov in 1997, it marked a turning point not just for AI but also for the chess world. Kasparov later collaborated with AI tools to pioneer "centaur chess," where humans and machines work together, combining intuition with raw computational power.

Comparing AI to Past Tech Revolutions

To put AI's growth into perspective, let's compare it to other major technological revolutions:

- **The Internet Era (1997–2002)**: Just as the internet reshaped communication and commerce, AI is transforming how we interact with information and automate tasks.
- **The Smartphone Boom (2007–2012)**: Smartphones put the internet in everyone's pocket. Similarly, today's AI tools are putting powerful capabilities in the hands of everyday users.

What's Next?

The journey of AI is far from over. With innovations happening every day, the possibilities are endless. From healthcare to education, AI's impact is growing rapidly, and we're all part of this exciting transformation. The rise of concepts like Artificial General Intelligence (AGI) suggests a future where AI could achieve human-like reasoning, bringing both opportunities and challenges.

In the next chapter, we'll dive into the mechanics of AI—how it works and how it powers the tools we use every day. Don't worry; we'll keep it simple and approachable!

04 How AI Works

AI might sound like a complex mystery, but it's surprisingly intuitive when you break it down. In this chapter, we'll demystify how AI operates and explain the concepts behind the tools you're already using—without diving into the deep end of technical jargon.

Simplifying Large Language Models (LLMs)

At the heart of many AI tools, including ChatGPT, is something called a **Large Language Model (LLM)**. Here's a simple way to think about it:

Imagine walking into the world's largest library and asking the librarian, "Can you recommend a book about space travel for kids?" The librarian doesn't just grab a random book; they use their knowledge of genres, age-appropriate content, and even popular titles to give you a spot-on recommendation. That's essentially how LLMs work—they analyze your request, search through vast amounts of information, and deliver an answer tailored to your needs.

But instead of books, LLMs process words, phrases, and contexts to predict the best response. They're trained on diverse datasets—everything from classic literature to online discussions. The more data they're trained on, the better they get at understanding and answering questions. This is why tools like ChatGPT can generate everything from detailed technical explanations to lighthearted jokes.

Natural Language Understanding (NLU)

Another key component of AI is **Natural Language Understanding (NLU)**. This is what allows AI tools to comprehend and respond to human language. Here's what NLU does:

- **Sentiment Analysis**: Determining if your input is positive, negative, or neutral. For example, if you type "I love pizza," the AI knows it's a positive sentiment.
- **User Intent Recognition**: Figuring out what you're trying to achieve. If you say, "Book a table for two," the AI understands that you want a restaurant reservation.
- **Contextual Understanding**: Keeping track of the conversation so responses make sense. For example, if you ask, "What's the weather like?" and then follow up with, "What about tomorrow?" the AI knows you're still talking about the weather.

NLU is a blend of linguistics, computer science, and machine learning. It powers applications ranging from customer service chatbots to advanced voice assistants.

Capabilities in Plain Terms

Here are a few real-world capabilities of AI systems like ChatGPT and beyond:

- **Generating Text**: Writing emails, essays, or even poems.
- **Answering Questions**: Providing quick answers based on vast knowledge.
- **Summarizing Information**: Condensing long articles or reports into bite-sized summaries.
- **Translation**: Converting text between languages seamlessly.
- **Personalization**: Offering tailored recommendations, like movie picks or shopping suggestions.
- **Creative Collaboration**: AI can assist in brainstorming, scriptwriting, or even creating music and art.

How AI Learns: Training and Feedback

AI systems don't just "know" things—they learn. Here's how:

1. **Training**: AI models are fed enormous amounts of data, like books, articles, and websites. This data helps the AI recognize patterns and build an understanding of language.
2. **Fine-Tuning**: After training, developers fine-tune the model for specific tasks, like answering questions or generating code. This makes AI more specialized and accurate for its intended use.

3. **Feedback**: AI systems improve through feedback. For example, when users rate responses or correct mistakes, the system learns to do better next time. Feedback loops are crucial for refining AI's performance and ensuring relevance.

The Role of Algorithms and Data

Behind every AI system is a set of algorithms—step-by-step instructions that tell the AI how to process data. Think of algorithms as recipes, guiding AI systems to identify patterns, make predictions, and generate responses. Data serves as the ingredients for these recipes. The quality, diversity, and quantity of data determine how effective and reliable the AI will be.

Limitations of AI

As impressive as AI is, it's not perfect. Here are a few common limitations:

- **Lack of Common Sense**: AI can't always make logical leaps that humans find obvious.
- **Dependence on Data**: If the training data is outdated or biased, the AI's responses might be flawed.
- **Creativity Boundaries**: While generative AI can produce creative outputs, it sometimes struggles with originality.
- **Understanding Nuance**: AI may misinterpret subtle cues like sarcasm or humor.
- **Overconfidence in Errors**: AI can sometimes present incorrect answers with great confidence, making it hard to spot mistakes.

Ethical Considerations

As AI becomes more integrated into our lives, ethical considerations are essential. How do we ensure that AI systems respect privacy, avoid bias, and remain transparent? Developers and users alike must address these questions to ensure responsible AI use.

Bringing It All Together

AI works by combining powerful algorithms with mountains of data to mimic human-like understanding. It processes language, recognizes patterns, and learns from feedback to become more effective over time. Tools like ChatGPT, Claude, and Gemini use these principles to power everything from casual chats to professional reports.

In the next chapter, we'll explore how you can harness these capabilities in your personal and professional life. Get ready to see AI in action!

05 Enhancing Your Personal Life with AI

Imagine having a personal assistant who's always on call, never forgets a task, and works faster than you could ever dream. That's what AI can feel like when you start using it in your everyday life. From saving time to sparking creativity, AI has countless ways to make your personal life easier, more enjoyable, and even more exciting.

Fun and Time-Saving Applications

Let's look at some of the simple yet powerful ways AI can enhance your daily routine:

- **Meal Planning**: Struggling to figure out what's for dinner? AI-powered apps can suggest recipes based on what's in your fridge, plan balanced meals for the week, and even generate a shopping list. Some tools can even customize meal plans for dietary restrictions or preferences, like vegan, keto, or gluten-free diets. Advanced apps may also integrate calorie tracking and nutrition insights to help you maintain a healthy lifestyle.

Sample Prompt for ChatGPT: "I have chicken, broccoli, and rice in my fridge. Can you suggest a simple and healthy dinner recipe using these ingredients? Also, include preparation steps and cooking time."

Another Prompt: "Plan a week of keto-friendly meals for a family of four, including a grocery list."

- **Personalized Entertainment**: Whether it's recommending your next Netflix binge or curating a playlist on Spotify, AI gets to know your tastes and delivers exactly what you want. AI can even analyze your viewing history to suggest hidden gems or new genres to explore. Some platforms now offer AI-curated movie nights, pairing films with food or drink recommendations.

  Sample Prompt for ChatGPT: "Can you recommend three Netflix movies that are similar to 'The Social Network' and 'Moneyball'?"

  Another Prompt: "Create a playlist of upbeat songs for a morning workout routine."

- **Event Planning**: Planning a birthday party or a family gathering? AI can help you brainstorm themes, design digital invitations, and even schedule reminders for RSVPs. Tools like Canva make it easy to create eye-catching graphics, while apps like Trello can help you organize tasks and timelines. Advanced AI assistants can even manage vendor communication, ensuring your event goes off without a hitch.

Sample Prompt for ChatGPT: "I'm hosting a birthday party for a 10-year-old who loves dinosaurs. Can you suggest a theme, decoration ideas, and a fun game for the kids?"

Another Prompt: "Help me draft a digital invitation for a family reunion, including date, time, and RSVP details."

AI as a Creative Partner

AI isn't just about doing the heavy lifting—it can also help you explore your creative side. Here's how:

- **Writing Assistant**: Tools like ChatGPT can help you draft poems, short stories, or even heartfelt messages for loved ones. Need a clever caption for Instagram? AI's got your back. For aspiring authors, AI can act as a brainstorming partner or even a rough editor. Some tools are designed specifically for creative writing, offering prompts, story arcs, or character suggestions.

- **Art and Design**: Generative AI platforms like DALL-E or Canva can help you create stunning visuals, whether you're designing a holiday card, experimenting with digital art, or conceptualizing a home renovation project. Some tools even allow you to print your creations directly onto products like mugs or T-shirts, turning your digital art into tangible keepsakes.

- **Idea Generation**: Whether you're brainstorming a new hobby, coming up with ideas for a DIY project, or planning a vacation itinerary, AI can help spark your imagination with unique and innovative suggestions. Some platforms even offer collaborative brainstorming features, allowing you to refine and expand on your initial ideas interactively.

Stress-Reducing Tools

Life can be hectic, but AI can help you stay organized and reduce stress:

- **Time Management**: Calendar apps powered by AI can suggest the best times for meetings, remind you of upcoming deadlines, and even block time for focused work. Some tools integrate with your email and task management systems for a seamless experience. AI can also identify patterns in your schedule, helping you optimize your day for productivity.
- **Fitness and Wellness**: AI-powered fitness apps can recommend personalized workout plans, track your progress, and even offer mindfulness exercises to help you relax. Wearable devices like Fitbits or Apple Watches use AI to monitor your health metrics and suggest improvements. Some apps even include guided meditation sessions tailored to your stress levels or goals.
- **Smart Assistants**: Devices like Alexa, Google Assistant, and Siri can handle mundane tasks like setting reminders, checking the weather, or even controlling your smart home. With voice commands, you can turn on lights, adjust the thermostat, or play your favorite music. Advanced assistants can now sync across devices, creating a seamless smart home experience.

Real-Life Examples

To see AI's impact in action, let's look at a few relatable scenarios:

1. **The Busy Parent**: Sarah uses an AI meal-planning app to organize dinners for her family of four. It suggests recipes, generates shopping lists, and even syncs with her grocery delivery service. On busy nights, she relies on voice-activated assistants to help manage her schedule and keep the kids entertained with educational games.
2. **The Hobbyist**: Mike, an amateur photographer, uses an AI editing tool to enhance his photos, turning casual snapshots into professional-quality images. He also uses generative AI to create unique backgrounds and overlays for his photos, giving them a creative edge. Recently, he started using AI tools to organize his portfolio, making it easier to share his work online.
3. **The Party Planner**: Emma is hosting a themed party and turns to AI for help. It suggests decoration ideas, writes a quirky invitation, and even creates a playlist to match the theme. She uses a voice assistant to set reminders and ensure everything stays on track. Emma also uses an AI budgeting tool to keep her expenses in check while planning the event.
4. **The DIY Enthusiast**: Jack wants to redecorate his living room. He uses AI design tools to visualize different furniture layouts, color schemes, and lighting options before making a single purchase. Jack also leverages AI-powered shopping assistants to find the best deals on furniture and décor items.
5. **The Lifelong Learner**: Anna, who loves learning new skills, uses AI to explore hobbies like cooking, painting, and playing the guitar. She relies on AI-powered language apps to learn Spanish and uses AI-generated video tutorials to improve her techniques in various crafts.

Getting Started

Here's how you can start integrating AI into your personal life today:

1. **Choose a Focus Area**: What's one task you'd love to make easier—meal planning, staying organized, or exploring a creative hobby?
2. **Pick a Tool**: Explore popular AI-powered apps in that area. For example, try ChatGPT for writing, Canva for design, or Alexa for organization.
3. **Experiment and Learn**: Don't worry about getting it perfect. AI tools are designed to adapt and improve as you use them. Start small and gradually explore more advanced features.

Unlocking More Possibilities

AI is a powerful ally for simplifying your life and enhancing your creativity. The more you explore, the more you'll discover new ways to make everyday tasks easier and more enjoyable. Whether you're managing a household, pursuing hobbies, or finding time for self-care, AI can be a transformative tool in your personal life.

In the next chapter, we'll dive into how AI can supercharge your professional workflow. Get ready to take productivity to the next level!

06 Supercharging Your Professional Workflow

Imagine having an assistant who works 24/7, never misses a deadline, and can instantly provide you with insights, suggestions, or polished content. That's what AI can bring to your professional life. In this chapter, we'll explore how AI can streamline your work, boost productivity, and help you focus on what really matters.

Beyond Google: AI's Edge in Instant Answers

We all love Google, but AI tools take information gathering to the next level. Instead of searching through multiple links, AI can:

- **Summarize complex topics**: Condense long articles or reports into bite-sized summaries in seconds.

- **Provide step-by-step guides**: Offer clear instructions for completing tasks, from technical setups to creative projects.
- **Generate tailored reports**: Deliver insights that are customized to your specific questions or needs.

For example, instead of reading five articles on a topic, you could ask an AI tool to summarize the key points for you in a single paragraph. This can save hours of research and help you make informed decisions faster.

Real-World Use Cases

Here are some practical ways AI can enhance your professional workflow:

- **Writing Emails**: Drafting emails can be time-consuming, especially when you're trying to strike the right tone. AI-powered tools like ChatGPT can draft, edit, or even rewrite emails in seconds.
  Example: Need to send a follow-up email after a meeting? AI can generate a professional, concise draft that you can tweak and send. Try prompts like, "Draft a follow-up email thanking a client for their time and summarizing key points discussed."
- **Preparing Presentations**: Whether it's creating slides or finding data, AI tools can speed up the process. For example, you can use AI to:
  - Design visually appealing slides with tools like Canva or Beautiful.ai.
  - Suggest bullet points based on your input.

- Summarize data into charts or graphs, making it easier to present complex information clearly.
- **Streamlining Project Management**: AI-powered platforms like Notion or Trello use intelligent automation to:
  - Set reminders for upcoming deadlines.
  - Assign tasks to team members based on workload.
  - Generate progress reports with minimal effort.
  - Offer predictive analytics to forecast project outcomes and potential bottlenecks.
- **Data Analysis**: Tools like Tableau and Google Data Studio leverage AI to:
  - Visualize data trends with dynamic charts and graphs.
  - Generate actionable insights from large datasets.
  - Provide predictive analytics for decision-making.

Case Studies: Professionals Using AI

To make these ideas more concrete, here are some examples of how professionals are using AI:

1. **The Sales Representative**: Maria uses AI to analyze customer data and generate personalized pitches, increasing her sales conversion rates. AI tools also provide her with real-time insights into customer behavior and preferences.
2. **The Freelancer**: John, a graphic designer, uses generative AI to brainstorm creative ideas and produce rough drafts for clients faster than ever. Tools like MidJourney help him visualize concepts, while Grammarly ensures his communication is clear and professional.

3. **The Manager**: Priya uses an AI-powered project management tool to organize her team's tasks, ensuring nothing falls through the cracks. She also uses sentiment analysis tools to gauge team morale and adapt her leadership strategies accordingly.
4. **The Educator**: Lisa, a teacher, leverages AI to create personalized lesson plans for her students. AI tools help her track student progress and recommend resources tailored to individual learning styles.

Tools to Get You Started

Here's a quick look at some popular AI tools you can use right now:

- **ChatGPT**: Ideal for drafting emails, brainstorming ideas, and answering questions quickly.
- **Gemini**: A powerful AI tool integrated into Chrome for summarizing and simplifying complex information.
- **Claude**: Excels at creating professional documents and summarizing long texts.
- **Grammarly**: Perfect for improving grammar, tone, and clarity in your writing.
- **Notion AI**: Combines note-taking with powerful automation and organization features.
- **Jasper AI**: Ideal for generating marketing content, blog posts, or even ad copy.
- **Tableau**: Helps analyze and visualize data, making reports easy to understand.
- **Synthesia**: Allows you to create professional-looking videos using AI avatars and voiceovers.

- **Otter.ai**: An excellent tool for transcribing meetings, generating notes, and keeping track of key points.

Tips for Integrating AI into Your Workflow

1. **Start Small**: Choose one task—like drafting emails or creating slides—and use AI to streamline it.
2. **Experiment**: Don't be afraid to try different tools to see which ones fit your style and needs.
3. **Balance AI with Human Touch**: While AI can save time, adding a personal touch to your work ensures it remains authentic and impactful.
4. **Stay Curious**: AI tools are constantly evolving. Keep exploring new features and updates to get the most out of them.
5. **Set Clear Goals**: Define what you want to achieve with AI, whether it's saving time, enhancing creativity, or improving accuracy.

The Future of Work with AI

AI isn't just a trend; it's a fundamental shift in how we work. By automating repetitive tasks and providing instant insights, AI allows you to focus on what you do best—whether that's creative thinking, problem-solving, or building relationships. As AI continues to advance, its role in professional settings will only grow, offering even more opportunities to innovate and excel.

In the next chapter, we'll dive into the practical steps for getting started with specific AI tools like ChatGPT and Gemini. Get ready to roll up your sleeves and put AI to work!

07 Getting Started with ChatGPT

By now, you've seen how powerful AI can be, and you're ready to take the next step—getting hands-on with ChatGPT. Whether you're looking to boost productivity, explore creativity, or simply have some fun, ChatGPT is an incredibly versatile tool. In this chapter, we'll guide you through setting up an account, understanding its features, and making the most of its capabilities.

What is ChatGPT?

Released in 2020 by OpenAI, ChatGPT is a conversational AI model designed to understand and generate human-like text. It's built on OpenAI's groundbreaking GPT (Generative Pre-trained Transformer) architecture, which uses advanced machine learning techniques to process and generate natural language. GPT excels at understanding context, predicting text, and providing coherent, meaningful responses. With ChatGPT, OpenAI aimed to create an AI that's as accessible as it is powerful, making it a go-to tool for productivity, creativity, and problem-solving.

Setting Up ChatGPT

Getting started with ChatGPT is easy, even if you're not tech-savvy. Here's how to do it:

1. **Visit the Website**: Head over to chat.openai.com to access ChatGPT.
2. **Create an Account**: Sign up using an email address or link your Google or Microsoft account.
3. **Choose a Plan**: ChatGPT offers free and paid options. The free version is perfect for beginners, while the paid version (ChatGPT Plus) unlocks advanced features like faster responses and access to the latest models.
4. **Start Chatting**: Once you're logged in, you can begin typing prompts in the chatbox. The AI will respond almost instantly.

Free vs. Paid Versions

Here's a quick breakdown of what each version offers:

- **Free Version**: Access to GPT-3.5, great for general queries and tasks.
- **Paid Version**: Access to GPT-4, which provides more advanced reasoning, creativity, and problem-solving abilities.

If you're unsure which to choose, start with the free version to get a feel for the tool. You can always upgrade later.

Understanding the Interface

The ChatGPT interface is simple and user-friendly. Here's what you'll see:

- **Chat Window**: This is where the conversation happens. Type your prompts here.
- **Conversation History**: On the left side, you'll see a list of your previous chats, allowing you to revisit past discussions.
- **Settings**: You can adjust preferences, explore new features, and manage your subscription.

Beginner Exercises

To get the hang of ChatGPT, try these beginner-friendly prompts:

1. **Ask a Question**: "What are some quick dinner recipes?"
2. **Plan Your Day**: "Help me create a schedule for a busy Monday."
3. **Write an Email**: "Draft a professional email to request a meeting with a client."
4. **Generate Ideas**: "Suggest 10 creative blog post topics for a travel website."

Everyday ChatGPT Prompts with Sample Responses

ChatGPT isn't just for work; it can assist with everyday tasks too. Here are some example prompts and responses:

1. **Meal Planning**:
   - **Prompt**: "I have chicken, spinach, and rice in my fridge. What can I make for dinner?"
   - **Response**: "You could make a delicious chicken and spinach stir-fry served over rice. Here's a simple recipe: Sauté garlic and onions in a pan, add diced chicken until cooked through, toss in spinach until wilted, and serve over steamed rice. Add soy sauce or spices for flavor!"

2. **Personalized Entertainment**:
   - **Prompt**: "Recommend a Netflix series similar to 'Stranger Things.'"
   - **Response**: "If you enjoyed 'Stranger Things,' you might like 'Dark' (a suspenseful sci-fi series) or 'The Umbrella Academy' (a quirky superhero drama with a mysterious twist)."

3. **Event Planning**:
   - **Prompt**: "I'm hosting a baby shower. Can you suggest a theme, menu, and a fun activity?"
   - **Response**: "How about a 'Storybook' theme? Decorate with fairy tale-inspired decor, serve finger foods like tea sandwiches and cupcakes, and for an activity, have guests create personalized storybook pages for the baby!"

4. **Fitness Goals**:
   - **Prompt**: "Design a beginner-friendly workout plan for someone who can exercise 3 days a week."

- Response: "Here's a simple plan: Day 1 - 20 minutes of brisk walking and 10 minutes of bodyweight exercises (squats, push-ups, and planks). Day 2 - 30 minutes of yoga or stretching. Day 3 - 15 minutes of light jogging and 15 minutes of strength training with dumbbells."

5. **Travel Tips**:
   - **Prompt**: "What are the must-see attractions in Paris for a 3-day trip?"
   - **Response**: "Day 1: Visit the Eiffel Tower, explore the Champs-Élysées, and enjoy the Arc de Triomphe. Day 2: Tour the Louvre, stroll through Jardin des Tuileries, and enjoy dinner at a Seine-side café. Day 3: Discover Montmartre, see Sacré-Cœur, and explore local art galleries."

6. **Shopping Assistance**:
   - **Prompt**: "I need a birthday gift idea for a friend who loves hiking."
   - **Response**: "Consider a lightweight backpack, a high-quality water bottle, or a hiking guidebook for scenic trails. If they like tech, a portable solar charger or GPS watch could be perfect!"

Advanced Features

Once you're comfortable, explore some of ChatGPT's more advanced capabilities:

- **Vision Capabilities**: With the ability to analyze uploaded content, ChatGPT takes AI interaction to the next level. Examples include:

- ○ **Image Analysis**: Upload a photo and ask ChatGPT to describe its contents, identify objects, or suggest improvements for photography.
- ○ **Document Review**: Upload PDFs or text documents, and ChatGPT can summarize, extract key points, or analyze the data for you.
- ○ **Charts and Graphs**: Share an image of a graph or chart, and ChatGPT can help interpret the data or explain trends.
- **Code Assistance**: Ask it to debug, explain, or even write simple code snippets.
- **Language Translation**: Translate phrases or entire paragraphs into multiple languages.
- **Creative Writing**: Collaborate on short stories, poems, or even scripts.

Troubleshooting Common Issues

Even the best tools have their quirks. Here's how to handle common issues:

- **Misunderstood Prompts**: Rephrase your question or break it into smaller steps.
- **Error Messages**: These can occur if the system is overloaded. Try refreshing the page or coming back later.
- **Unexpected Results**: If the response seems off, provide more context or clarify your intent.
- **Limitations**: Remember, ChatGPT doesn't "know" everything. It generates responses based on patterns in its training data, which may lead to inaccuracies.

Tips for Success

- **Be Specific**: The clearer your input, the better the output.
- **Use Follow-Up Prompts**: If the first answer isn't quite right, ask for clarification or refinement.
- **Experiment**: Don't be afraid to try new types of prompts. ChatGPT is designed to handle a wide range of topics and tasks.

The Power of ChatGPT

ChatGPT isn't just a tool; it's a gateway to endless possibilities. Whether you're brainstorming ideas, tackling professional tasks, or exploring personal projects, it adapts to your needs. The more you use it, the better you'll understand how to make it work for you.

In the next chapter, we'll take a closer look at Gemini, another powerful AI tool that's redefining productivity and creativity. Stay tuned!

08 Getting Started with Gemini

If ChatGPT is your conversational powerhouse, Gemini is your all-in-one AI productivity tool, seamlessly integrated into your browser to enhance everyday tasks. Whether you're researching a project, organizing information, or simplifying complex topics, Gemini is designed to help you work smarter, not harder. Let's dive into how you can get started with Gemini and make the most of its capabilities.

What is Gemini?

Released in 2023 by Google, Gemini is an advanced AI tool designed to integrate seamlessly into your browsing experience. It combines the power of natural language processing with real-time data analysis to simplify and enhance your online tasks. Gemini is particularly useful for anyone looking to summarize, organize, and make sense of large amounts of web content efficiently.

Gemini is more than just a passive assistant—it actively works alongside you as you browse. Integrated into platforms like Google Chrome, it operates in the background to summarize, simplify, and analyze web content, providing instant insights without disrupting your workflow. It's like having a research assistant that's always ready to help.

Setting Up Gemini

Getting started with Gemini is straightforward. Here's how to do it:

1. **Install the Extension**: Go to the Chrome Web Store and search for "Gemini AI" to add the extension to your browser.
2. **Create an Account**: Sign up using your email or social login to unlock all features.
3. **Customize Settings**: Tailor Gemini to your needs by adjusting preferences, like the type of summaries you want or the level of detail in its analyses.
4. **Start Browsing**: Once installed, Gemini will automatically activate when you're visiting compatible web pages, offering suggestions and insights in real time.

Use Cases for Beginners

Gemini is easy to use, even for beginners. Here are some practical ways to get started:

- **Summarizing Articles**: Found an interesting but lengthy article? Gemini can condense it into key takeaways, saving you time while ensuring you don't miss the main points.

- **Simplifying Research**: Whether you're working on a school project or exploring a complex topic, Gemini can highlight the most relevant sections of a webpage and suggest further reading.
- **Organizing Information**: Use Gemini to create summaries or bullet points from dense content, making it easier to digest and share.
- **Bookmarking Insights**: Save key findings directly in Gemini for future reference, ensuring your research stays organized.

Advanced Features

Once you're comfortable with the basics, try out these advanced features:

- **Interactive Highlights**: Highlight text on a webpage, and Gemini will provide context, explanations, or related information. This feature is especially useful for understanding technical jargon or unfamiliar concepts.
- **Multi-Page Analysis**: Gemini allows you to gather insights across multiple tabs or pages without jumping back and forth. It consolidates information into a single summary, streamlining your workflow.
- **AI-Driven Suggestions**: Receive personalized recommendations for related topics, resources, or tools based on your browsing history and queries.
- **Language Translation**: Translate content directly on the page, making multilingual research effortless. This is particularly helpful for global projects or learning new languages.

- **Collaboration Tools**: Share summaries or notes with colleagues directly through Gemini, fostering seamless teamwork.

Everyday Prompts and Scenarios

Gemini is designed to handle a wide range of tasks. Here are some examples of prompts and how it can respond:

1. **Research Assistance**:
   - **Prompt**: "Summarize this article about climate change in three key points."
   - **Response**: "1) Global temperatures are rising due to greenhouse gas emissions. 2) Urgent action is needed to reduce carbon footprints. 3) Renewable energy adoption is critical for sustainability."
2. **Project Preparation**:
   - **Prompt**: "Create bullet points summarizing this report on marketing trends."
   - **Response**: Gemini highlights key insights, such as "Social media advertising saw a 30% increase in ROI," and "Video content remains the most engaging format."
3. **Understanding Data**:
   - **Prompt**: "Explain the trends in this graph about economic growth."
   - **Response**: Gemini provides an analysis, noting increases, plateaus, or declines and offering potential reasons behind the trends.
4. **Translation on the Fly**:

- **Prompt**: "Translate this article about robotics from German to English."
- **Response**: Gemini delivers a clear and accurate translation directly on the page, maintaining the original format.

Practical Examples of Gemini in Action

To see Gemini's power in real life, here are some scenarios:

1. **The Student**: Emma is researching climate change for a class project. She uses Gemini to summarize articles, extract key statistics, and organize notes, cutting her research time in half. Gemini also suggests additional resources, helping her build a comprehensive bibliography.
2. **The Professional**: Raj is preparing for a client presentation. With Gemini, he highlights key data points from multiple reports and converts them into a polished summary to share with his team. Gemini also recommends visual aids, such as charts or graphs, to enhance his presentation.
3. **The Writer**: Carla is drafting a blog post about emerging technologies. Gemini helps her identify credible sources, summarize technical details, and organize her ideas into an outline, making her writing process more efficient.
4. **The Language Learner**: Alex is learning Spanish and uses Gemini to translate articles and provide vocabulary explanations. Gemini's instant translations and contextual insights accelerate his language-learning journey.

Tips for Success

- **Explore Shortcuts**: Use Gemini's keyboard shortcuts to speed up tasks like summarizing or translating content.
- **Experiment with Preferences**: Customize how Gemini displays summaries or insights to fit your workflow.
- **Combine Tools**: Pair Gemini with ChatGPT for an unbeatable combination—use Gemini for research and ChatGPT for brainstorming or drafting.
- **Stay Organized**: Take advantage of Gemini's note-saving feature to keep all your insights in one place.

Why Gemini?

Gemini is more than just an AI assistant; it's a productivity partner that helps you navigate the web with ease. By simplifying information and streamlining your workflow, Gemini lets you focus on what matters most. Whether you're a student, a professional, or a curious learner, Gemini adapts to your needs and makes complex tasks manageable.

In the next chapter, we'll explore Claude, another incredible AI tool designed for professional tasks and detailed projects. Stay tuned to see how it can take your productivity to the next level!

09 Exploring Claude

If ChatGPT and Gemini are powerful tools for general tasks, Claude by Anthropic is your go-to AI for professional and complex projects. Designed with a focus on safety, transparency, and reliability, Claude excels at tasks that require detailed analysis, polished outputs, and professional-level capabilities. In this chapter, we'll guide you through getting started with Claude and showcase how it can elevate your productivity.

What is Claude?

Claude is an AI-powered assistant developed by Anthropic, a company dedicated to creating safe and interpretable AI systems. Named after Claude Shannon, the "father of information theory," this tool is designed to assist with tasks that demand precision and professionalism. Released in 2023, Claude is particularly adept at understanding nuanced instructions, crafting detailed documents, and summarizing complex materials.

What sets Claude apart is its commitment to safety and transparency. Anthropic has built Claude with safeguards to reduce biases, ensure reliability, and maintain high-quality outputs, making it a trusted tool for professional environments.

Setting Up Claude

Getting started with Claude is simple:

1. **Access the Platform**: Visit Anthropic's website or use Claude through integrated platforms where it's available.
2. **Create an Account**: Sign up using an email address or log in with a supported account.
3. **Explore the Interface**: Claude's intuitive interface makes it easy to start crafting, editing, or analyzing content right away.
4. **Choose a Plan**: Like many AI tools, Claude offers both free and premium options, with the premium version providing access to more advanced features and higher usage limits.

Use Cases for Claude

Claude shines in a variety of professional applications. Here are a few examples:

- **Document Creation**: Craft comprehensive reports, proposals, or presentations with minimal effort. Claude can generate drafts, refine content, and ensure a professional tone.

- **Summarization**: Perfect for condensing lengthy reports, research papers, or meeting notes into clear and concise summaries.
- **Data Analysis**: Input datasets or spreadsheets, and Claude can help you identify trends, create summaries, or even draft insights for presentations.
- **Professional Communication**: Write polished emails, client proposals, or marketing content that aligns with your goals.
- **Brainstorming**: Use Claude to generate ideas for campaigns, project plans, or problem-solving strategies.

Everyday Prompts and Examples

To get a better sense of how Claude can assist you, here are some prompts and sample responses:

1. **Drafting Proposals**:
   - **Prompt**: "Draft a project proposal for implementing a new customer feedback system. Include objectives, benefits, and a timeline."
   - **Response**: "Objective: Implement a streamlined feedback system to improve customer satisfaction by 25% within six months. Benefits: Real-time feedback collection, data-driven insights, and enhanced customer retention. Timeline: Phase 1 - Research (2 weeks), Phase 2 - System Implementation (6 weeks), Phase 3 - Monitoring and Optimization (4 weeks)."
2. **Summarizing Reports**:
   - **Prompt**: "Summarize this 20-page market analysis report into five key points."

- Response: Claude condenses the report into actionable insights, such as "1) Market demand for eco-friendly products is growing by 18% annually. 2) Competitor X has captured 35% of the market share. 3) Key demographics include millennials aged 25-40."

3. **Data Insights**:
   - **Prompt**: "Analyze this dataset and highlight three key trends in sales performance over the last quarter."
   - **Response**: "1) Sales increased by 15% in urban areas compared to rural regions. 2) Product Y saw a 25% rise in popularity during holiday promotions. 3) Customer retention rates improved by 10% after implementing loyalty rewards."

4. **Email Writing**:
   - **Prompt**: "Write a follow-up email to a client, thanking them for their time and outlining next steps."
   - **Response**: "Subject: Thank You for Your Time - Next Steps

5. Dear [Client Name],
   Thank you for meeting with us earlier today. We greatly appreciate your insights and enthusiasm for the project. As discussed, our next steps include finalizing the project scope by [date] and scheduling a follow-up meeting to review the updated proposal. Please let us know your availability for next week. Looking forward to collaborating further.
   Best regards, [Your Name]"

Advanced Features

Once you're comfortable with the basics, explore Claude's more advanced functionalities:

- **Custom Templates**: Create reusable templates for recurring tasks, like project proposals or status reports. Save time by standardizing processes.
- **Collaboration Tools**: Claude supports collaborative workflows, making it easy to share drafts, gather feedback, and refine documents with team members.
- **Integration Capabilities**: Use Claude with other productivity tools like Slack, Notion, or project management platforms to streamline your workflow.
- **Code Assistance**: Claude can analyze code, debug scripts, and even suggest improvements for software projects.

Practical Examples of Claude in Action

Here's how professionals use Claude to streamline their workflows:

1. **The Project Manager**: Sarah uses Claude to draft detailed project plans and generate progress updates for stakeholders. With Claude's help, she saves hours every week and ensures her reports are polished and professional.
2. **The Data Analyst**: Alex uploads raw data into Claude, which identifies trends, drafts insights, and even creates visual summaries for team presentations. Alex pairs Claude with Tableau for dynamic data visualizations.

3. **The Marketing Specialist**: Emily leverages Claude to brainstorm campaign ideas, write ad copy, and polish client-facing reports. Claude's ability to tailor content to specific audiences makes her marketing materials more impactful.
4. **The Educator**: Michael uses Claude to summarize research papers for his lectures, create detailed lesson plans, and draft academic articles for publication.

Tips for Success

- **Start with Clear Prompts**: The more specific you are, the better Claude can meet your needs. Include as much detail as possible when describing your task.
- **Iterate and Refine**: Use follow-up prompts to refine outputs until they're just right.
- **Leverage Integrations**: Explore how Claude can work alongside your existing tools to create a seamless workflow.
- **Experiment with Templates**: Build custom templates to standardize repetitive tasks.

Why Choose Claude?

Claude is a professional powerhouse that combines precision with ease of use. Its advanced capabilities make it an ideal choice for anyone working on detailed projects or managing complex workflows. By focusing on safety and reliability, Claude ensures you can trust it with your most critical tasks.

In the next chapter, we'll explore other generative AI tools that can enhance your productivity and creativity. From video creation to personal branding, there's a tool for everyone!

10 Other Popular Generative AI Tools

While ChatGPT, Gemini, and Claude are powerful tools for specific tasks, the world of generative AI offers even more possibilities. From creating videos to designing professional branding, there's an AI tool for almost every need. In this chapter, we'll explore some of the most popular and innovative generative AI tools available today, along with their key features, use cases, and practical examples to inspire your creativity.

Tools for Video Creation: Synthesia

What it Does: Synthesia enables you to create professional-looking videos using AI avatars and voiceovers. Instead of filming yourself or hiring actors, you can use Synthesia to produce polished video content effortlessly.

Best Use Cases:

- Training and onboarding videos.
- Marketing content for products and services.
- Personal video messages or announcements.

Example: Imagine you're creating an onboarding video for new employees. With Synthesia, you can generate a professional video with a virtual presenter explaining company policies, complete with text overlays and branding.

Advanced Features:

- Customizable avatars with branding options.
- Multi-language support for global audiences.
- Integration with scriptwriting tools for seamless video creation.

Tools for Note-Taking and Transcription: Otter.ai

What it Does: Otter.ai is an AI-powered transcription tool that converts spoken words into text in real time. It's perfect for meetings, lectures, and brainstorming sessions.

Best Use Cases:

- Transcribing meeting notes.
- Capturing lecture content for students.
- Generating searchable records of brainstorming sessions.

Example: A team leader uses Otter.ai during a project meeting to create an instant transcript, allowing the team to focus on discussions rather than taking notes.

Advanced Features:

- Speaker identification for multi-person meetings.
- Keyword summaries for quick navigation.
- Integration with platforms like Zoom and Microsoft Teams.

Tools for Art and Design: MidJourney/DALL-E

What it Does: These AI platforms generate stunning artwork and visuals from text prompts. Whether you're a designer, marketer, or hobbyist, these tools help bring your creative ideas to life.

Best Use Cases:

- Concept art for projects.
- Social media graphics and promotional materials.
- Personal creative exploration.

Example: A content creator uses DALL-E to design unique, eye-catching thumbnails for YouTube videos based on their video topics.

Advanced Features:

- High-resolution outputs for professional use.
- Style customization to match specific aesthetics.
- Iterative refinement for perfecting artwork.

Tools for Writing and Content Creation: Jasper AI

What it Does: Jasper AI specializes in generating marketing content, blog posts, social media copy, and more. With customizable templates, it helps you create compelling content tailored to your needs.

Best Use Cases:

- Crafting ad copy.
- Writing SEO-optimized blog posts.
- Generating ideas for social media campaigns.

Example: A small business owner uses Jasper AI to draft Instagram captions and ad copy for a new product launch, saving hours of creative work.

Advanced Features:

- Tone adjustments to match brand voice.
- Content optimization for SEO.
- Automated brainstorming for fresh ideas.

Tools for Personal Branding: Headshot Generators

What it Does: These tools use AI to generate professional-looking headshots based on your uploaded photos. They're perfect for creating a polished online presence.

Best Use Cases:

- LinkedIn profile pictures.
- Marketing and personal branding materials.
- Team pages for company websites.

Example: A job seeker uploads a casual photo to a headshot generator and receives a professional, retouched portrait suitable for their LinkedIn profile.

Advanced Features:

- Background editing and lighting adjustments.
- Style presets for corporate or casual looks.
- Multi-format downloads for web and print.

Tools for Workflow Automation: Zapier and Make

What They Do: These platforms use AI to automate repetitive tasks and integrate multiple apps into a seamless workflow. They're invaluable for businesses and individuals looking to save time and increase efficiency.

Best Use Cases:

- Automating data entry across platforms.
- Syncing customer relationship management (CRM) systems.
- Managing social media posts.

Example: A marketer uses Zapier to automatically post new blog content to social media platforms, saving time and ensuring consistency.

Advanced Features:

- Multi-step workflows for complex automation.
- Integration with hundreds of apps and platforms.
- Conditional logic to tailor processes to specific scenarios.

Additional Tools to Explore

- **Canva**: A design platform powered by AI to create graphics, presentations, and videos.
- **Runway ML**: A tool for creating videos, animations, and visual effects using AI.
- **Copy.ai**: An AI-driven writing assistant tailored for ad copy, blog posts, and more.
- **Grammarly**: Enhances writing with grammar checks, tone adjustments, and clarity improvements.

Choosing the Right Tool

With so many options available, how do you decide which tools to use? Here are some tips:

1. **Define Your Needs**: Identify what tasks you want to simplify or enhance.
2. **Try Free Versions**: Many tools offer free tiers or trials—explore them before committing.

3. **Combine Tools**: Use multiple AI tools together for maximum efficiency. For example, pair Otter.ai for meeting notes with Jasper AI for drafting follow-up emails.
4. **Focus on Integration**: Choose tools that work well with your existing systems to avoid disruptions.

The Expanding World of Generative AI

Generative AI is constantly evolving, and new tools are being developed every day. Whether you're a student, a professional, or simply curious, there's never been a better time to explore these innovative technologies. Each tool offers unique capabilities that can enhance your creativity, productivity, and overall workflow.

Practical Tips for Success

- **Experiment and Learn**: Don't hesitate to explore different tools to find the perfect match for your needs.
- **Stay Updated**: Follow industry news to discover new tools and features.
- **Invest in Training**: Learning to use these tools effectively can significantly boost your productivity and creativity.

In the next chapter, we'll guide you through interactive exercises to help you try these tools firsthand. Get ready to unleash your creativity and see what AI can do for you!

11 You Try It!

Now that you've explored a wide range of AI tools, it's time to roll up your sleeves and put them to work. This chapter is all about interactive exercises and activities that will help you experience the power of AI firsthand. Whether you're curious, creative, or looking to streamline your daily life, these exercises will spark ideas and build confidence in using AI tools.

Activity 1: Ask ChatGPT for a Dinner Recipe

One of the simplest ways to start with AI is by asking ChatGPT for a personalized dinner recipe. Here's how:

1. Open ChatGPT and type: "I have chicken, broccoli, and rice. Can you suggest a quick and healthy dinner recipe?"
2. Observe the detailed recipe it generates, including preparation steps and cooking time.

3. Optional: Ask ChatGPT for substitutions or variations, such as vegetarian or gluten-free options.

Expand the Activity:

- Ask ChatGPT to create a meal plan for the week, complete with grocery lists.
- Request tips for meal prepping or ingredient substitutions to save money.

This exercise shows how AI can quickly provide practical solutions for everyday challenges.

Activity 2: Generate Creative Email Drafts

AI tools can take the hassle out of writing emails. Try this:

1. Use ChatGPT or Claude to draft an email. Type: "I need a polite email to thank a client for their feedback and schedule a follow-up meeting."
2. Review the draft and make edits if needed.
3. Experiment with different tones—professional, casual, or friendly.

Expand the Activity:

- Ask AI to craft a response to a tricky email, such as a client complaint or a delayed delivery.
- Generate multiple variations of the same email to find the tone that suits your audience best.

You'll see how AI can save time and inspire polished communication.

Activity 3: Plan a Weekend Itinerary

Need help planning a getaway? Let Gemini or ChatGPT assist:

1. Type: "Plan a 2-day itinerary for a weekend trip to New York City, focusing on art and food."
2. Review the suggested schedule, including museum visits and top-rated restaurants.
3. Ask follow-up questions to customize your itinerary, like "What's the best time to visit MoMA?"

Expand the Activity:

- Request budget-friendly options for accommodations and activities.
- Add specific preferences, like "Include family-friendly activities" or "Focus on outdoor attractions."

This activity highlights how AI can act as a personal travel planner, tailoring recommendations to your needs.

Activity 4: Create Stunning Visuals

Explore the creative side of AI with tools like DALL-E or MidJourney:

1. Open the tool and enter a prompt like: "A serene beach at sunset with a futuristic city skyline in the background."
2. Observe the generated visuals and download your favorite.

3. Experiment with different prompts to explore various styles and themes.

Expand the Activity:

- Create a series of images based on a theme, like fantasy landscapes or futuristic technology.
- Use the visuals in social media posts, presentations, or personal projects.

This is perfect for creating artwork for personal or professional use.

Activity 5: Transcribe and Summarize Notes

Use Otter.ai to simplify note-taking and transcription:

1. Record a short brainstorming session or meeting.
2. Upload the recording to Otter.ai and watch as it transcribes your speech into text.
3. Use the summarized notes to outline key points and action items.

Expand the Activity:

- Share the transcript with team members and use Otter.ai's collaboration tools to assign tasks.
- Highlight keywords or phrases for easy navigation.

Activity 6: Draft a Blog Post with Jasper AI

For aspiring writers or content creators, Jasper AI can jump-start your blog writing:

1. Enter a topic like: "Top 5 benefits of using AI for small businesses."
2. Review the AI-generated draft and add your personal touch.
3. Use Jasper's SEO tools to ensure your post is optimized for search engines.

Expand the Activity:

- Ask Jasper to generate headlines or subheadings for your post.
- Request follow-up ideas for a blog series based on your initial topic.

Activity 7: Create a Video with Synthesia

Explore video creation with Synthesia:

1. Choose a virtual avatar and script a short message, such as: "Welcome to our company! Here's what you need to know about our values and mission."
2. Generate the video and download the final product.
3. Use this for onboarding, marketing, or personal projects.

Expand the Activity:

- Add multiple scenes with different avatars to create a dynamic presentation.
- Experiment with multi-language support for global audiences.

Activity 8: Automate a Workflow with Zapier

Use Zapier to automate a repetitive task:

1. Identify a task, such as posting new blog content to social media.
2. Create a Zap that connects your blog platform to your social media accounts.
3. Test the automation and watch it work seamlessly.

Expand the Activity:

- Use Zapier to integrate multiple apps, like syncing CRM data with email campaigns.
- Explore conditional logic to create more complex workflows.

Reflect on Your AI Experience

After trying these exercises, take a moment to reflect:

- Which tools did you find most useful or enjoyable?
- What surprised you about using AI?
- How could you integrate these tools into your personal or professional life?

Next Steps

The best way to learn AI is by doing. As you experiment with these tools, you'll uncover new possibilities and gain confidence in harnessing AI's potential. In the next chapter, we'll explore real-life examples of how AI has transformed the author's daily routines and career. Get ready for inspiring stories and practical insights!

12 Next Steps in Your AI Journey

Congratulations! You've reached the final chapter of this book and taken your first big steps into the exciting world of Artificial Intelligence. By now, you've learned what AI is, explored its applications, and even experimented with some powerful tools. But your journey doesn't end here—this is just the beginning. In this chapter, we'll discuss how to continue learning, applying, and growing with AI in your personal and professional life.

Embrace a Lifelong Learning Mindset

AI is a rapidly evolving field, with new developments happening almost daily. Staying informed and adaptable is key to making the most of this technology. Here's how to keep learning:

- **Follow AI News and Trends**:
    - Subscribe to newsletters like *The AI Newsletter* or *OpenAI Updates* for regular insights.

- Follow thought leaders and organizations on platforms like LinkedIn, Twitter, or YouTube to stay updated on breakthroughs and applications.
- Explore podcasts like *AI in Business* or *The AI Alignment Podcast* to hear experts discuss trends and future directions.
- **Take Online Courses**:
  - Platforms like Coursera, Udemy, and edX offer courses on AI and machine learning tailored for beginners, such as "AI for Everyone" by Andrew Ng.
  - Dive deeper with specialized topics like natural language processing (NLP) or computer vision.
  - OpenAI's documentation and tutorials provide hands-on guidance for exploring tools like ChatGPT or OpenAI Codex.
- **Experiment with New Tools**:
  - Stay curious and test new AI tools as they emerge. Many offer free trials or beginner-friendly interfaces.
  - Use platforms like Product Hunt or AI directories to discover trending AI technologies.

Apply AI to Your Life and Career

AI's potential isn't limited to tech experts. Here are some practical ways to integrate AI into your daily routines and career:

- **Boost Productivity**:
  - Automate repetitive tasks with tools like Zapier or Make to save time and reduce errors.

- Use AI assistants like ChatGPT or Claude to draft emails, create summaries, or brainstorm ideas.
- Explore scheduling tools powered by AI, like Motion, to optimize your calendar.

- **Enhance Creativity**:
  - Explore generative AI tools like MidJourney, DALL-E, or Synthesia to design visuals, write stories, or produce videos.
  - Use AI for brainstorming sessions, whether for work projects, personal hobbies, or creative writing.
  - Collaborate with AI tools to refine music compositions, edit videos, or generate innovative product ideas.

- **Expand Your Skills**:
  - Develop expertise in using AI tools specific to your industry, such as Tableau for data visualization, Grammarly for polished writing, or Canva's AI-powered design features.
  - Consider joining workshops or webinars to deepen your understanding of AI's applications in areas like marketing, data science, or customer service.

Stay Mindful of AI's Ethical Implications

As you incorporate AI into your life, it's important to remain mindful of its ethical considerations. Here are some guidelines:

- **Protect Privacy**:

- Be cautious about sharing sensitive data with AI tools. Review privacy policies to understand how your data is stored and used.
- Use secure platforms that prioritize user data protection and comply with regulations like GDPR or CCPA.
- **Address Bias**:
    - Recognize that AI models may have inherent biases based on their training data. Always review AI-generated outputs critically.
    - Advocate for inclusivity and fairness in AI development and deployment.
- **Use AI Responsibly**:
    - Ensure that the AI tools you use align with ethical practices and do not harm others.
    - Educate yourself about the societal impacts of AI, such as job displacement and misinformation, to use it thoughtfully.

Build a Community

You don't have to navigate your AI journey alone. Joining a community of like-minded individuals can provide support, inspiration, and new opportunities:

- **Online Forums and Groups**:
    - Platforms like Reddit (e.g., r/MachineLearning or r/ArtificialIntelligence) or Discord communities are great places to ask questions and share ideas.
    - Participate in social media groups dedicated to AI discussions and learning.

- **Local Meetups**:
    - Many cities host AI-focused meetups or hackathons where you can network, learn, and collaborate on projects.
    - Check platforms like Meetup.com for events in your area.
- **Professional Organizations**:
    - Consider joining groups like the Association for the Advancement of Artificial Intelligence (AAAI) or IEEE to connect with professionals in the field.
    - Attend conferences like NeurIPS, CES, or AI Expo to gain insights and expand your network.

Imagine Your AI-Enhanced Future

As you move forward, think about how AI can shape your future. Here are some questions to reflect on:

- How can AI streamline your daily tasks or help you achieve your personal goals?
- What new career opportunities could arise from mastering AI tools?
- How can AI help you tackle creative challenges or explore new hobbies?

AI is a powerful tool to help you achieve your goals. The more you experiment and adapt, the more you'll discover its endless possibilities. Keep pushing boundaries and exploring how AI can enhance your life.

A Final Word

AI is more than just a technology—it's a catalyst for transformation, innovation, and growth. By embracing it, you're not just keeping up with the times; you're stepping into the future. Remember, the journey is yours to shape. Keep exploring, keep experimenting, and most importantly, keep learning.

Thank you for taking this journey with us. Here's to unlocking the full potential of Artificial Intelligence and making it an integral part of your life and career!

13 Resources for Continued Learning

To continue your journey into the world of artificial intelligence, it's essential to engage with reputable resources that deepen your understanding and keep you updated on the latest developments. Below is a curated list of books, blogs, online courses, and podcasts, with URLs written out for easy access.

Books

1. **Artificial Intelligence: A Guide to Intelligent Systems** by Michael Negnevitsky
   A beginner-friendly introduction to AI concepts, including problem-solving and neural networks.
2. **Life 3.0: Being Human in the Age of Artificial Intelligence** by Max Tegmark
   Explores the future of AI and its impact on society, ethics, and humanity.
3. **Prediction Machines: The Simple Economics of Artificial Intelligence** by Ajay Agrawal, Joshua Gans, and Avi Goldfarb

Examines how AI impacts decision-making and business strategy.

4. **AI Superpowers: China, Silicon Valley, and the New World Order** by Kai-Fu Lee
A look at the global AI race, particularly the competition between the U.S. and China.

5. **Deep Learning Illustrated** by Jon Krohn, Grant Beyleveld, and Aglaé Bassens
A visually engaging guide to deep learning concepts for beginners.

6. **Genesis: Artificial Intelligence, Hope, and the Human Spirit** by Henry Kissinger, Eric Schmidt, and Daniel Huttenlocher
An exploration of how artificial intelligence is reshaping humanity's understanding of knowledge, decision-making, and ethics in a rapidly evolving world.
URL: https://a.co/d/i3metp1

Blogs

1. **OpenAI Blog**
Insights and updates from one of the leading AI research organizations.
URL: https://openai.com/blog

2. **Towards Data Science**
Articles on AI, machine learning, and data science written by experts and enthusiasts.
URL: https://towardsdatascience.com

3. **AI Alignment Forum**
Discussions and research on the ethical and safe

development of AI.
URL: https://www.alignmentforum.org

4. **MIT Technology Review: AI Section**
News and analysis of the latest trends and breakthroughs in AI.
URL:
https://www.technologyreview.com/topic/artificial-intellige
nce/

5. **The Gradient**
In-depth AI research summaries, interviews, and opinion pieces.
URL: https://thegradient.pub

6. **AI Wars**
A comprehensive article detailing the evolution of AI and the companies driving innovation in the space.
URL:
https://www.hbs.edu/faculty/Pages/item.aspx?num=63881

Online Courses

1. **Machine Learning** by Stanford University (Coursera)
A popular introduction to machine learning taught by Andrew Ng, covering supervised and unsupervised learning.
URL: https://www.coursera.org/learn/machine-learning

2. **Elements of AI** by Reaktor and the University of Helsinki
A free online course designed to make AI accessible to everyone.
URL: https://www.elementsofai.com

3. **AI For Everyone** by Andrew Ng (Coursera)
A non-technical overview of AI, focusing on how it's

transforming industries and how to adopt it in your work.
URL: https://www.coursera.org/learn/ai-for-everyone

4. **Introduction to Artificial Intelligence** (edX)
A comprehensive course covering AI concepts, algorithms, and real-world applications.
URL:
https://www.edx.org/course/cs50s-introduction-to-artificial-intelligence-with-python

5. **Deep Learning Specialization** by Andrew Ng (Coursera)
A series of courses diving deep into neural networks, convolutional networks, and sequence models.
URL:
https://www.coursera.org/specializations/deep-learning

6. **Google Cloud Free AI Courses**
Learn the basics of AI, machine learning, and data analysis with free courses from Google Cloud.
URL: https://www.cloudskillsboost.google/

Podcasts

1. **Talking Machines**
A podcast covering the latest research and applications of machine learning and AI.
URL: https://www.thetalkingmachines.com

2. **The AI Alignment Podcast**
Explores the ethical and philosophical dimensions of AI development.
URL: https://futureoflife.org/ai-alignment-podcast/

3. **AI in Business**
Discusses how businesses are leveraging AI for growth and

innovation.
URL: https://www.emerj.com/podcast

4. **Data Skeptic**
    Focuses on AI, data science, and machine learning, with
    insights for both beginners and experts.
    URL: https://dataskeptic.com

Additional Resources

-   **Google AI Education**
    A hub of free resources, tools, and courses to understand AI
    and its applications.
    URL: https://ai.google/education/

-   **Fast.ai**
    Free online courses and tools to help beginners understand
    deep learning and AI.
    URL: https://www.fast.ai

These resources provide a variety of ways to deepen your
understanding of AI, whether through engaging books, insightful
blogs, or interactive online courses. Choose what resonates with
your learning style and dive in to continue your AI journey!

14 Case Studies: Real-Life Examples of AI in Action

Artificial intelligence is transforming industries and solving problems in ways we couldn't have imagined just a few years ago. Here are some real-life examples of AI in action, demonstrating its versatility and power across different sectors.

1. Healthcare: Early Detection of Diseases

Case Study: AI-Powered Cancer Diagnosis

- **The Challenge**: Detecting cancer in its early stages is critical for effective treatment, but traditional methods can be time-consuming and prone to error.
- **The AI Solution**: Google's DeepMind developed an AI system that analyzes mammograms to identify signs of

breast cancer. The model was trained on thousands of images to detect abnormalities with high accuracy.

- **The Impact**: The AI system reduced false positives by 5.7% and false negatives by 9.4%, helping doctors make more accurate diagnoses and save lives.
- **Takeaway**: AI's ability to process vast amounts of medical data can enhance diagnostic accuracy and efficiency, giving healthcare professionals more time to focus on patient care.

2. Retail: Personalized Shopping Experiences

Case Study: Amazon's Recommendation Engine

- **The Challenge**: Offering customers personalized recommendations at scale.
- **The AI Solution**: Amazon uses AI algorithms to analyze customer browsing history, purchase patterns, and product reviews. The system suggests products tailored to individual preferences.
- **The Impact**: Amazon's recommendation engine accounts for approximately 35% of its total sales, demonstrating the power of personalization in driving revenue.
- **Takeaway**: AI-driven personalization not only enhances the customer experience but also boosts sales by connecting shoppers with products they're likely to buy.

3. Transportation: Autonomous Vehicles

Case Study: Tesla's Autopilot System

- **The Challenge**: Developing vehicles that can navigate roads safely without human intervention.
- **The AI Solution**: Tesla's Autopilot leverages neural networks, cameras, sensors, and real-time data processing to enable semi-autonomous driving. The system can detect obstacles, maintain lane positioning, and even respond to traffic signals.
- **The Impact**: Tesla's Autopilot has logged millions of miles, advancing the development of self-driving technology while reducing human error—a leading cause of accidents.
- **Takeaway**: AI in transportation is reshaping mobility, with potential benefits for safety, efficiency, and accessibility.

4. Agriculture: Sustainable Farming Practices

Case Study: John Deere's AI-Powered Equipment

- **The Challenge**: Increasing crop yields while minimizing resource usage.
- **The AI Solution**: John Deere developed AI-driven agricultural equipment that uses computer vision to detect weeds and precisely spray herbicides only where needed.
- **The Impact**: Farmers reduced herbicide usage by up to 90%, saving money and reducing environmental impact.
- **Takeaway**: AI can help optimize resource usage in agriculture, promoting sustainability while maintaining productivity.

5. Entertainment: Enhancing Creativity

Case Study: Netflix's Content Recommendations

- **The Challenge**: Keeping viewers engaged by offering relevant content in a highly competitive streaming market.
- **The AI Solution**: Netflix uses AI to analyze viewing habits, user ratings, and behavioral data to recommend shows and movies tailored to individual preferences.
- **The Impact**: Personalized recommendations contribute to higher viewer retention, with 80% of watched content driven by AI suggestions.
- **Takeaway**: AI can personalize entertainment experiences, keeping audiences engaged and increasing customer loyalty.

6. Financial Services: Fraud Detection

Case Study: Mastercard's AI Fraud Detection System

- **The Challenge**: Identifying fraudulent transactions quickly to minimize financial losses.
- **The AI Solution**: Mastercard uses machine learning models to analyze transaction patterns in real time, flagging anomalies that might indicate fraud.
- **The Impact**: The system processes 75 billion transactions annually, identifying and preventing millions of fraudulent activities.
- **Takeaway**: AI's ability to analyze data in real time makes it a valuable tool for enhancing security and protecting consumers.

7. Education: Personalized Learning

Case Study: Duolingo's Language Learning Platform

- **The Challenge**: Providing personalized, effective language instruction to millions of users worldwide.
- **The AI Solution**: Duolingo's AI adapts lessons to each user's skill level, learning pace, and areas of difficulty. The platform uses natural language processing to evaluate pronunciation and offer feedback.
- **The Impact**: Duolingo has over 500 million users, making language learning accessible and effective for people of all ages.
- **Takeaway**: AI can democratize education by delivering personalized and scalable learning experiences.

8. Climate Change: Environmental Monitoring

Case Study: Microsoft's AI for Earth Program

- **The Challenge**: Tackling environmental challenges such as deforestation, water scarcity, and wildlife conservation.
- **The AI Solution**: Microsoft provides grants and AI tools to organizations working on environmental projects. For example, AI-powered satellite imagery analysis helps detect illegal deforestation in real time.
- **The Impact**: Conservation efforts have become more efficient and targeted, aiding in the preservation of ecosystems.
- **Takeaway**: AI can play a critical role in combating climate change and promoting sustainability.

9. Small Businesses: Automating Customer Support

Case Study: Chatbots for Small Retailers

- **The Challenge**: Providing timely customer support with limited resources.
- **The AI Solution**: Small businesses use AI-powered chatbots like Tidio to handle common customer inquiries, recommend products, and resolve issues.
- **The Impact**: Businesses improve response times, reduce operational costs, and enhance customer satisfaction.
- **Takeaway**: AI democratizes access to advanced tools, enabling small businesses to compete with larger companies.

10. Public Safety: Predictive Policing

Case Study: Crime Analysis with PredPol

- **The Challenge**: Preventing crime by allocating law enforcement resources more effectively.
- **The AI Solution**: PredPol uses historical crime data to predict where crimes are likely to occur, enabling proactive policing.
- **The Impact**: Law enforcement agencies report reductions in crime rates by focusing patrols on high-risk areas.
- **Takeaway**: AI can enhance public safety, though it must be implemented ethically to avoid bias and over-policing.

11. Supply Chain Optimization

Case Study: DHL's AI-Powered Logistics

- **The Challenge**: Managing complex supply chains to ensure timely deliveries.
- **The AI Solution**: DHL uses AI to optimize delivery routes, predict demand, and automate warehouse operations.
- **The Impact**: Reduced operational costs, faster delivery times, and increased customer satisfaction.
- **Takeaway**: AI can transform logistics, making global supply chains more efficient and resilient.

12. Urban Planning: Smart Cities

Case Study: Barcelona's Smart City Initiative

- **The Challenge**: Managing urban growth and improving city services.
- **The AI Solution**: Barcelona integrates AI into its city infrastructure, using sensors and data analytics to optimize traffic flow, reduce energy consumption, and enhance public services.
- **The Impact**: Improved quality of life for residents and a more sustainable urban environment.
- **Takeaway**: AI can revolutionize urban planning, creating smarter and more sustainable cities.

These case studies highlight the transformative potential of AI across industries. Whether it's improving healthcare outcomes, enhancing creativity, or promoting sustainability, AI is helping us solve complex challenges and create new opportunities. The possibilities are vast, and these real-world applications are just the beginning.

15 Predictions for the Future of AI

Artificial Intelligence is evolving at an unprecedented pace, and its potential to reshape industries, societies, and even daily life is both exciting and profound. In this chapter, we'll explore predictions for how AI might develop over the next two decades, offering insights into its possible impacts and opportunities.

The Next 2 Years: Widespread Adoption and Specialization

- **Consumer Applications**: AI tools will become even more embedded in daily life, from smarter virtual assistants to AI-driven personalized health apps that track and predict wellness needs.
- **Generative AI Evolution**: Tools like ChatGPT, Gemini, and Claude will become more accessible, integrating deeper multimodal capabilities, such as combining text, images, and even video into cohesive outputs.

- **Workforce Augmentation**: AI will continue to assist professionals by automating repetitive tasks, streamlining workflows, and providing enhanced analytical capabilities. Remote work tools will leverage AI to create virtual environments that feel increasingly realistic and collaborative.
- **Ethical Frameworks**: Governments and organizations will begin implementing more robust regulations and guidelines for ethical AI use, addressing concerns like bias, transparency, and data privacy.

The Next 5 Years: Transformational Shifts

- **AI-Driven Industries**:
  - **Healthcare**: AI will revolutionize diagnostics, drug discovery, and personalized treatment plans, improving patient outcomes globally.
  - **Education**: Adaptive learning platforms will tailor educational experiences to individual students' needs, promoting lifelong learning and closing knowledge gaps.
  - **Transportation**: Autonomous vehicles will likely see broader adoption, reducing accidents and reshaping urban planning by freeing up parking spaces and optimizing traffic flow.
- **Hyper-Personalization**: AI will enhance everything from entertainment (e.g., fully personalized movies and games) to shopping experiences (e.g., virtual fitting rooms and predictive recommendations).

- **Collaboration with Humans**: AI systems will work alongside humans in creative and decision-making roles, becoming collaborators rather than mere tools.

The Next 10 Years: A New AI Ecosystem

- **General Artificial Intelligence (AGI)**: While still speculative, early stages of AGI may emerge, capable of performing a wide range of intellectual tasks with minimal human input.
- **Universal Connectivity**: AI will power interconnected devices in smart cities, homes, and workplaces, creating seamless and intelligent environments that adapt to human needs in real time.
- **Decentralized AI**: With advances in blockchain and edge computing, decentralized AI systems will allow users to retain greater control over their data and AI interactions, enhancing privacy and transparency.
- **New Professions**: Entirely new career paths will emerge around AI ethics, training, and maintenance, as well as roles that blend human creativity with AI capabilities, such as "AI experience designers."

The Next 20 Years: A Reshaped World

- **Radical Advancements in AGI and the Path to Superintelligence**: If AGI (Artificial General Intelligence) is realized, it could lead to systems capable of reasoning, learning, and adapting across all domains at or beyond human levels. The leap to Superintelligence—an AI surpassing human cognitive abilities in virtually every aspect—could redefine human civilization, transforming science, technology, art, and philosophy.

Superintelligence: The Ultimate Frontier

- **Potential Benefits of Superintelligence**:
  - **Solving Global Challenges**: From eradicating diseases to reversing climate change, a Superintelligent AI could address humanity's most pressing issues with unmatched efficiency and insight.
  - **Scientific Breakthroughs**: Theoretical physics, medicine, and even space exploration could advance at unprecedented speeds under the guidance of a Superintelligent AI.
  - **Optimized Resource Management**: Superintelligence could revolutionize agriculture, energy, and logistics, ensuring sustainability and equitable resource distribution worldwide.
- **Risks and Ethical Challenges**:
  - **Loss of Control**: Once Superintelligence emerges, ensuring human oversight could become increasingly challenging. How do we align its objectives with humanity's well-being?
  - **Existential Risks**: Unintended actions or goals by a Superintelligent AI could pose catastrophic consequences if misaligned with human values.
  - **Ethical Considerations**: Questions about AI rights, human autonomy, and the balance between innovation and safety will dominate discussions.
- **Preparing for Superintelligence**:

- Alignment Research: Ensuring that Superintelligent AI aligns with human values and ethics is a critical research area.
- Global Collaboration: Governments, organizations, and AI developers must work together to establish frameworks and safeguards.
- Public Awareness: Educating society about Superintelligence's potential impacts fosters informed discussions and decision-making.

The Expanding Role of AI in Society

- **Human-AI Integration**: Technologies like brain-computer interfaces could enable direct communication between humans and AI, blurring the lines between biological and artificial intelligence.
- **Global Problem Solving**:
  - Climate Change: AI will optimize resource management, energy efficiency, and environmental restoration efforts.
  - Healthcare: Diseases that are currently untreatable may become manageable or eradicated through AI-driven medical breakthroughs.
- **Ethical and Philosophical Challenges**: The rise of AGI will raise profound questions about what it means to be human, the role of work, and the balance between progress and ethical considerations.

Opportunities and Challenges

While the potential of AI is boundless, it's not without challenges. As AI advances, we'll need to:

- Address ethical dilemmas, ensuring AI benefits all of humanity.
- Build robust frameworks for accountability and transparency.
- Prepare for economic shifts, such as job displacement and the creation of new industries.

Preparing for the Future

The best way to prepare for AI's future is to stay informed, adaptable, and proactive. By engaging with AI today, you'll be better positioned to leverage its opportunities and navigate its challenges as it continues to evolve.

A Final Thought

The future of AI is one of immense possibility. Over the next two decades, it will shape the world in ways we can only begin to imagine. Superintelligence, in particular, represents the apex of this evolution, offering profound opportunities while posing equally significant challenges. By embracing AI with curiosity, responsibility, and an open mind, we can ensure it becomes a force for good, enhancing lives and creating a better future for all.

16 Careers in AI

Artificial Intelligence is more than just a transformative technology—it's a booming industry offering exciting career opportunities. Whether you're a student, a professional looking to pivot, or someone eager to future-proof your career, AI provides a wealth of roles across industries. In this chapter, we'll explore the most in-demand AI careers, the skills you'll need, and how to get started.

Why Pursue a Career in AI?

The AI industry is growing rapidly, with applications spanning healthcare, finance, entertainment, and more. Here's why it's a great time to consider an AI-focused career:

- **High Demand**: Companies across all sectors need AI talent to stay competitive.
- **Lucrative Salaries**: AI professionals are among the highest-paid in tech.
- **Global Opportunities**: AI skills are in demand worldwide, offering roles in every region.
- **Diverse Applications**: From creative fields to technical ones, AI opens doors in various industries.
- **Impactful Work**: Careers in AI offer opportunities to solve global challenges, from climate change to healthcare accessibility.

Key Career Paths in AI

1. **Chief AI Officer**
   - **Role**: Lead an organization's AI strategy and implementation, ensuring alignment with business goals and ethical considerations.
   - **Skills**: Leadership, AI expertise, strategic planning, and knowledge of industry-specific AI applications.
   - **Industries**: Technology, finance, healthcare, retail, and any enterprise leveraging AI at scale.
2. **Data Scientist**
   - **Role**: Analyze and interpret complex data to provide actionable insights.
   - **Skills**: Python, R, SQL, machine learning, data visualization.
   - **Industries**: Finance, healthcare, retail, technology.
3. **Machine Learning Engineer**
   - **Role**: Design, build, and optimize machine learning models.

- Skills: Programming (Python, Java, C++), deep learning frameworks (TensorFlow, PyTorch).
- Industries: Technology, automotive, robotics, e-commerce.

4. **AI Research Scientist**
   - **Role**: Conduct advanced research to develop new AI algorithms and systems.
   - **Skills**: Mathematics, programming, theoretical computer science, research methodology.
   - **Industries**: Academia, technology R&D, government.

5. **AI Ethicist**
   - **Role**: Ensure AI systems are developed and deployed responsibly.
   - **Skills**: Knowledge of AI frameworks, ethics, philosophy, policy-making.
   - **Industries**: Government, NGOs, tech companies.

6. **Natural Language Processing (NLP) Specialist**
   - **Role**: Develop systems that process and understand human language.
   - **Skills**: Computational linguistics, machine learning, programming.
   - **Industries**: Customer service, content moderation, education.

7. **Robotics Engineer**
   - **Role**: Design and build robots powered by AI.
   - **Skills**: Robotics, engineering, machine learning, hardware design.
   - **Industries**: Manufacturing, healthcare, logistics.

8. **AI Product Manager**

- ○ **Role**: Oversee the development and deployment of AI-powered products.
- ○ **Skills**: Product management, AI basics, user experience (UX), project management.
- ○ **Industries**: Technology, consumer goods, media.

9. **AI Trainer or Annotator**
   - ○ **Role**: Train AI systems by labeling and categorizing data.
   - ○ **Skills**: Attention to detail, familiarity with AI tools.
   - ○ **Industries**: Tech startups, data-focused enterprises.

10. **AI Consultant**
    - ○ **Role**: Advise businesses on how to integrate AI solutions into their workflows and operations.
    - ○ **Skills**: Business acumen, AI knowledge, change management.
    - ○ **Industries**: Consulting, technology, finance, and healthcare.

Emerging Careers in AI

As AI continues to evolve, new roles are emerging:

- **AI Policy Advisor**: Work with governments and organizations to create regulations and frameworks for AI development.
- **AI Experience Designer**: Blend creativity and technical expertise to craft intuitive AI interactions, such as conversational interfaces and AI-driven user experiences.
- **AI Data Strategist**: Develop data strategies that align AI initiatives with business goals, ensuring efficient use of data resources.

Essential Skills for AI Careers

To thrive in the AI field, develop these core competencies:

- **Programming Skills**: Python, R, and Java are widely used in AI development.
- **Mathematics and Statistics**: A strong foundation in algebra, calculus, and probability is crucial.
- **Machine Learning**: Learn how to build, train, and deploy machine learning models.
- **Problem-Solving**: Critical thinking and creativity are essential for tackling AI challenges.
- **Domain Knowledge**: Understanding the industry you're working in (e.g., healthcare, finance) can set you apart.
- **Communication Skills**: The ability to explain complex AI concepts to non-technical stakeholders is invaluable.

How to Get Started

1. **Learn the Basics**:
   - Take online courses on platforms like Coursera, Udemy, or edX.
   - Study introductory AI and machine learning concepts through books or tutorials.
2. **Build Hands-On Experience**:
   - Complete projects, such as building a chatbot or analyzing datasets.
   - Participate in hackathons or join AI-focused open-source communities.
3. **Pursue Certifications and Degrees**:

- ○ Certifications in AI, data science, or machine learning can boost your resume.
  - ○ Consider degrees in computer science, data analytics, or related fields.
4. **Network**:
  - ○ Join professional groups like the Association for the Advancement of Artificial Intelligence (AAAI).
  - ○ Attend industry events, webinars, and local meetups.
5. **Stay Updated**:
  - ○ Follow AI news and trends to keep your skills relevant.
  - ○ Experiment with emerging tools and technologies.

The Future of AI Careers

As AI continues to evolve, new career paths will emerge, blending technical expertise with creativity, ethics, and leadership. The demand for AI professionals will grow, with industries seeking specialists who can bridge the gap between technology and real-world applications.

Final Thoughts

The possibilities in AI are vast and varied, offering opportunities for everyone, regardless of their background. Whether you're coding algorithms, creating ethical guidelines, or managing AI-powered projects, your work can help shape the future of technology and society. Now is the time to explore, experiment, and embark on your AI career journey!

Glossary of AI Terms

Artificial Intelligence can feel overwhelming with all its jargon and technical terms. This glossary is here to simplify things, giving you clear and concise explanations of the most common AI terms you'll encounter. By the end of this chapter, you'll feel confident navigating the AI world.

Artificial Intelligence (AI)

The field of computer science focused on creating machines capable of performing tasks that typically require human intelligence, such as learning, reasoning, and problem-solving.

Algorithm

A set of rules or instructions a computer follows to complete a task or solve a problem. In AI, algorithms process data to learn patterns and make predictions.

Machine Learning (ML)

A subset of AI that enables systems to learn and improve from experience without being explicitly programmed. Examples include recommendation systems and fraud detection algorithms.

Neural Network

A type of machine learning model inspired by the human brain. Neural networks consist of layers of interconnected nodes (neurons) that process and analyze data.

Deep Learning

A subset of machine learning that uses large neural networks with many layers (hence "deep") to analyze complex patterns in data. It's the technology behind image recognition and natural language processing.

Generative AI

A type of AI focused on creating new content, such as text, images, or music, based on patterns learned from existing data. Tools like ChatGPT and DALL-E are examples of generative AI.

Large Language Model (LLM)

A machine learning model trained on vast amounts of text data to understand and generate human-like language. ChatGPT is an example of an LLM.

Natural Language Processing (NLP)

The branch of AI that deals with the interaction between computers and human language. NLP enables machines to understand, interpret, and generate human language.

Training Data

The dataset used to teach an AI model. This data helps the model recognize patterns and make predictions. The quality of training data directly affects the model's performance.

Overfitting

When an AI model performs well on training data but struggles with new, unseen data. This happens when the model becomes too specialized to the training data.

Reinforcement Learning

A machine learning technique where an AI system learns by trial and error, receiving rewards for correct actions and penalties for incorrect ones. It's used in robotics and game-playing AI.

Supervised Learning

A type of machine learning where the model is trained on labeled data, meaning each input has a corresponding correct output. It's like learning with a teacher.

Unsupervised Learning

A type of machine learning where the model analyzes and identifies patterns in data without labeled outputs. It's used for clustering and anomaly detection.

Chatbot

An AI-powered program designed to simulate human conversation. Chatbots are commonly used for customer service, virtual assistants, and interactive experiences.

API (Application Programming Interface)

A set of tools and protocols that allow different software applications to communicate. AI APIs let developers integrate AI capabilities, like text generation or image recognition, into their apps.

Bias in AI

When an AI system produces unfair or prejudiced results due to biases present in its training data. Addressing bias is crucial for creating fair and ethical AI systems.

Prompt

The input or question given to an AI tool to generate a response. For example, asking ChatGPT, "What's a quick recipe for dinner?" is a prompt.

Token

A unit of text, such as a word or a character, used in AI language models to process and generate responses. Tokens are the building blocks of language for models like GPT.

Model Fine-Tuning

The process of adjusting a pre-trained AI model to perform better on specific tasks or datasets. Fine-tuning helps make AI tools more specialized and accurate.

Ethics in AI

The study and practice of ensuring AI systems are developed and used responsibly, addressing concerns like privacy, bias, and transparency.

GPT (Generative Pre-trained Transformer)

An advanced AI architecture that powers tools like ChatGPT. It's designed to generate coherent and contextually relevant text based on input prompts.

AI Winter

A period when progress and investment in AI slow down due to unmet expectations. Historically, there have been several "AI winters," but recent advancements have led to a resurgence.

Cloud Computing

The use of remote servers hosted on the internet to store, manage, and process data. Cloud computing is essential for running and scaling AI systems.

Explainability

The ability of an AI system to explain how it arrived at a decision or prediction. Explainability is important for building trust and understanding in AI systems.

The Singularity

A hypothetical future point when AI surpasses human intelligence, potentially leading to significant societal changes. While speculative, it's a popular topic in discussions about AI's future.

Generative Adversarial Network (GAN)

A type of neural network used for generating realistic images, videos, or audio. GANs consist of two models—a generator and a discriminator—that compete to improve outputs.

Conclusion

This glossary is your cheat sheet for understanding the key terms in AI. By familiarizing yourself with these concepts, you'll feel more confident navigating the world of artificial intelligence. Keep this chapter handy as a reference guide as you explore and experiment with AI tools!

References

Below is a curated list of references used throughout this book, including articles, reports, and other sources that provide reliable information about artificial intelligence and its applications. These references are organized by type for easy navigation.

Books

1. Tegmark, Max. *Life 3.0: Being Human in the Age of Artificial Intelligence*. Vintage, 2018.
2. Agrawal, Ajay, Joshua Gans, and Avi Goldfarb. *Prediction Machines: The Simple Economics of Artificial Intelligence*. Harvard Business Review Press, 2018.
3. Lee, Kai-Fu. *AI Superpowers: China, Silicon Valley, and the New World Order*. Houghton Mifflin Harcourt, 2018.
4. Negnevitsky, Michael. *Artificial Intelligence: A Guide to Intelligent Systems*. Pearson, 2005.

Articles and Reports

1. McKinsey Global Institute. *The State of AI in 2023*.
   URL:
   https://www.mckinsey.com/business-functions/mckinsey-digital/our-insights/the-state-of-ai-in-2023
2. Google AI. "AI for Social Good."
   URL: https://ai.google/social-good

3. OpenAI. "DALL·E: Creating Images from Text."
   URL: https://openai.com/dall-e
4. Harvard Business Review. "How AI Is Changing Work and
   Organizational Culture."
   URL:
   https://hbr.org/2023/02/how-ai-is-changing-work-and-orga
   nizational-culture
5. MIT Technology Review. "The Future of AI: Trends to
   Watch."
   URL: https://www.technologyreview.com

Websites and Blogs

1. OpenAI Blog.
   URL: https://openai.com/blog
2. Towards Data Science.
   URL: https://towardsdatascience.com
3. Microsoft AI for Earth.
   URL: https://www.microsoft.com/en-us/ai/ai-for-earth
4. Google AI Experiments.
   URL: https://experiments.withgoogle.com/ai
5. The Gradient.
   URL: https://thegradient.pub

Courses and Educational Resources

1. Coursera. "Machine Learning" by Andrew Ng (Stanford
   University).
   URL: https://www.coursera.org/learn/machine-learning

2. Elements of AI.
   URL: https://www.elementsofai.com
3. Khan Academy. "AI-Powered Lessons."
   URL: https://www.khanacademy.org
4. Deep Learning Specialization by Andrew Ng (Coursera).
   URL:
   https://www.coursera.org/specializations/deep-learning

Case Studies

1. Google DeepMind. "AI for Early Cancer Detection."
   URL: https://deepmind.com/research
2. Tesla. "Autonomous Driving Technology."
   URL: https://www.tesla.com/autopilot
3. Netflix Technology Blog. "Building the Recommendation
   Algorithm."
   URL: https://netflixtechblog.com
4. Microsoft AI Case Studies.
   URL: https://www.microsoft.com/en-us/ai/ai-case-studies

This references section offers reliable resources to explore further,
validate information, or deepen your understanding of AI.